W9-ACT-102

SCIENCE BEHIND THE COLORS
POISON FROGS

by Alicia Z. Klepeis

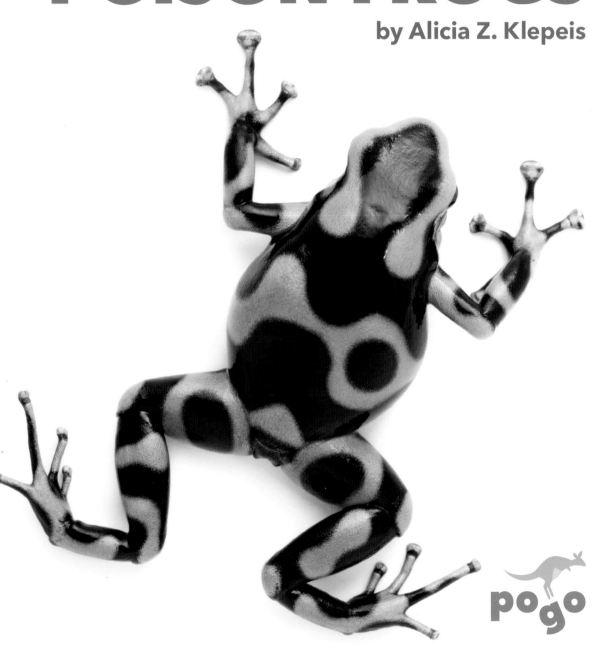

pogo

Ideas for Parents and Teachers

Pogo Books let children practice reading informational text while introducing them to nonfiction features such as headings, labels, sidebars, maps, and diagrams, as well as a table of contents, glossary, and index.

Carefully leveled text with a strong photo match offers early fluent readers the support they need to succeed.

Before Reading

- "Walk" through the book and point out the various nonfiction features. Ask the student what purpose each feature serves.
- Look at the glossary together. Read and discuss the words.

Read the Book

- Have the child read the book independently.
- Invite him or her to list questions that arise from reading.

After Reading

- Discuss the child's questions. Talk about how he or she might find answers to those questions.
- Prompt the child to think more. Ask: Did you know about the unique life cycle of a frog before reading this book? Do you know any other animals that go through life cycle changes?

Pogo Books are published by Jump!
5357 Penn Avenue South
Minneapolis, MN 55419
www.jumplibrary.com

Library of Congress Cataloging-in-Publication Data

Names: Klepeis, Alicia, 1971- author.
Title: Poison frogs / by Alicia Z. Klepeis.
Description: Pogo books edition.
Minneapolis, MN: Jump!, Inc., [2021]
Series: Science behind the colors | Includes index.
Audience: Ages 7-10 | Audience: Grades 2-3
Identifiers: LCCN 2020007431 (print)
LCCN 2020007432 (ebook)
ISBN 9781645275862 (hardback)
ISBN 9781645275879 (paperback)
ISBN 9781645275886 (ebook)
Subjects: LCSH: Dendrobatidae—Juvenile literature.
Classification: LCC QL668.E233 K58 2021 (print)
LCC QL668.E233 (ebook) | DDC 597.8/77—dc23
LC record available at https://lccn.loc.gov/2020007431
LC ebook record available at https://lccn.loc.gov/2020007432

Editor: Jenna Gleisner
Designer: Molly Ballanger

Photo Credits: Dirk Ercken/Shutterstock, cover, 4; kikkerdirk/iStock, 1, 3, 10-11br, 20-21; Daniel Borzynski/Alamy, 5; Rauschenbach/SuperStock, 6-7; Eric Isselee/Shutterstock, 8; slowmotiongli/Shutterstock, 9; Thorsten Spoerlien/iStock, 10-11tl; Ondrej Prosicky/Shutterstock, 10-11tr; Hotshotsworldwide/Dreamstime, 10-11bl; Thorsten Spoerlien/Shutterstock, 12-13; Art Wolfe Stock/Cultura Limited/SuperStock, 14-15; rod williams/Alamy, 16; Michael & Patricia Fogden/Minden Pictures/SuperStock, 17; Greg Basco/BIA/Minden Pictures/SuperStock, 18-19; PetlinDmitry/iStock, 23.

Printed in the United States of America at Corporate Graphics in North Mankato, Minnesota.

TABLE OF CONTENTS

CHAPTER 1
Pretty but Poisonous...................................4

CHAPTER 2
Bright Spots and Stripes......................8

CHAPTER 3
Toxic Tadpoles...............................16

ACTIVITIES & TOOLS
Try This!...22
Glossary...23
Index...24
To Learn More................................24

CHAPTER 1

PRETTY BUT POISONOUS

What creature can breathe on land and in water? This colorful **amphibian** is a poison frog! It can scare away **predators** with bright colors and poison.

Poison frogs are tiny. Most are about one inch (2.5 centimeters) long. That is about the size of a paperclip!

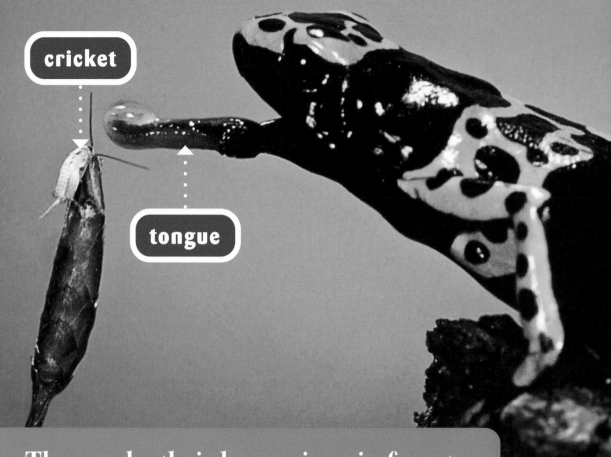

cricket

tongue

They make their homes in rain forests. Some live high in the trees. But most live among leaves on the forest floor. They leap and climb. Their sticky feet cling to trees and leaves. Their long, sticky tongues catch insects. These include beetles, ants, and crickets.

TAKE A LOOK!

· ·

Poison frogs live in rain forests in Central and South America. Take a look!

= where poison frogs live

N
W ⊕ E
S

CHAPTER 2

BRIGHT SPOTS AND STRIPES

Poison frogs' **genes** play the biggest role in giving them their colors. Layers of **pigments** in their skin mix to make their colors. Special **nanocrystals** can make their skin blue.

Bright colors help keep these frogs alive. How? They warn predators. They say, "Back off! I am poisonous!" The poison comes from the insects they eat. The brightest frogs are the most poisonous.

harlequin
poison frog

green and black
poison frog

strawberry
poison frog

three-striped
poison frog

Poison frogs come in many colors and **patterns**. Some have stripes. Others have spots. There are many colors within one **species**.

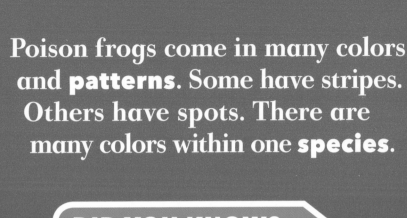

DID YOU KNOW?

Strawberry poison frogs are also called blue jeans frogs. Why? Their bright blue back legs make them look like they are wearing jeans!

Most frogs are active at night. But not poison frogs! They are most active during the day. Why? In daylight, predators can see their colors. A red or yellow frog stands out in the rain forest.

golden
poison frog

Some poison frogs' colors and patterns serve as **camouflage**. The dyeing poison dart frog is an example. It is bright yellow, blue, and black. Up close, these colors stand out. But from a distance, they blend in. They aren't as easy to see. This helps hide them from predators.

CHAPTER 3

TOXIC TADPOLES

Males croak to call for females. Colors help now, too. How? Females prefer to **mate** with brighter males. Bright colors are a sign of good health.

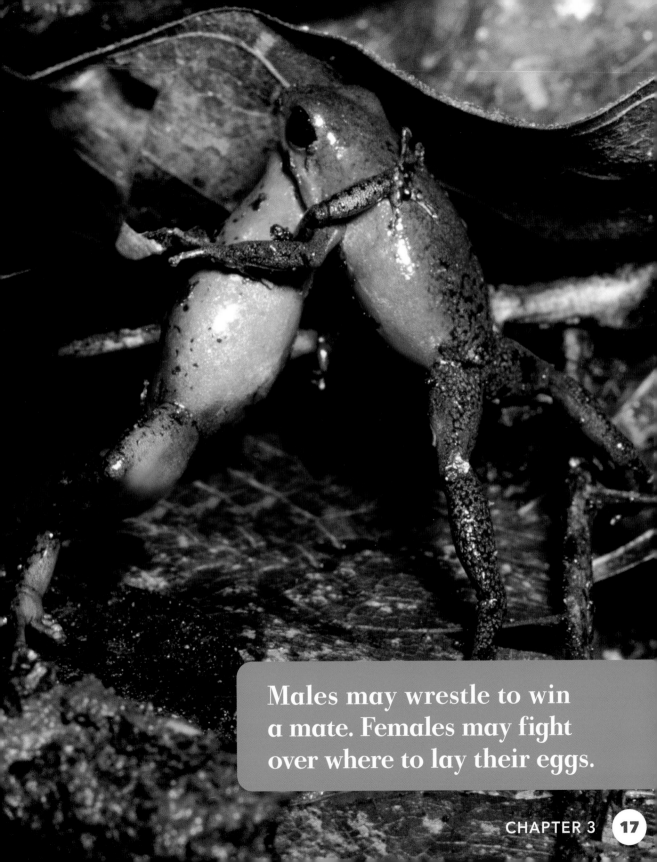

Males may wrestle to win a mate. Females may fight over where to lay their eggs.

New **tadpoles** are not bright like their parents. They are usually black. But even as babies, they are **toxic**. Both male and female poison frogs take care of their **offspring**. They will even carry them on their backs to water! Why? Tadpoles need water to live.

tadpoles

TAKE A LOOK!

All frogs have a unique life cycle. Take a look at the **stages**.

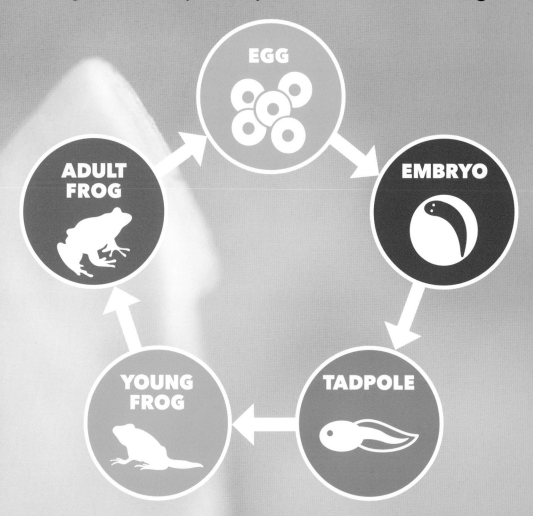

By the time a young frog has its legs, its coloring is similar to that of its parents. A poison frog is **mature** at about one year old. At this point, its color will be at its brightest. It will go on to stand out in the rain forest.

ACTIVITIES & TOOLS

ANIMAL LIFE CYCLES

Find out more about animal life cycles in this activity!

What You Need:

- computer or books and magazines
- small sheets of paper
- crayons, markers, or colored pencils
- tape or glue
- large sheet of paper or poster board

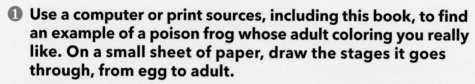

❶ Use a computer or print sources, including this book, to find an example of a poison frog whose adult coloring you really like. On a small sheet of paper, draw the stages it goes through, from egg to adult.

❷ Research again to find another example of an animal, such as a jellyfish or a ladybug, that goes through life cycle stages.

❸ Draw the life cycle of this other creature.

❹ Tape or glue your life cycle drawings to your poster board. If you have access to a printer, you could also print out pictures.

❺ How are the life stages of each animal similar or different?

GLOSSARY

amphibian: A cold-blooded animal with a backbone that lives in water and breathes with gills when young. As an adult, it develops lungs and lives on land.

camouflage: An animal's natural form or coloring that allows it to blend in with its surroundings.

genes: Parts of living things that are passed from parents to offspring and determine how one looks and grows.

mate: To join together to produce babies.

mature: Adult or fully grown.

nanocrystals: Very tiny solid substances inside a layer of cells that reflect blue or green light.

offspring: The young of animals, people, or plants.

patterns: Repeating arrangements of colors, shapes, or figures.

pigments: Substances that give color to something.

predators: Animals that hunt other animals for food.

species: One of the groups into which similar animals and plants are divided.

stages: Steps or periods of development.

tadpoles: Young frogs that live in water, breathe through gills, and have long tails but no legs.

toxic: Poisonous.

INDEX

amphibian 4

camouflage 15

colors 4, 8, 9, 11, 12, 15, 16, 20

dyeing poison dart frog 15

eggs 17, 19

feet 6

females 16, 17, 18

genes 8

golden poison frog 12

insects 6, 9

legs 11, 20

life cycle 19

males 16, 17, 18

mate 16, 17

nanocrystals 8

patterns 11, 15

pigments 8

poison 4, 9, 12

predators 4, 9, 12, 15

rain forests 6, 7, 12, 20

species 11

strawberry poison frogs 11

tadpoles 18, 19

tongues 6

water 4, 18

wrestle 17

TO LEARN MORE

Finding more information is as easy as 1, 2, 3.

1 Go to www.factsurfer.com

2 Enter "poisonfrogs" into the search box.

3 Click the "Surf" button to see a list of websites.

FACT
SURFER